'Love, the argument goes, is not a force that can be contained: Ed Carson's poems in *Taking Place* don't attempt to bind the un-bindable — they approximate love's flavour, turning outward to the other and inward to the self, and also wandering among love's mysteries, This meditation on love over time rewards re-reading: the reach for the divine is threaded through with human failings: these strike me as not only graceful, but truthful poems.'

— Marilyn Bowering, author of *What It Takes To Be Human*

'Edward Carson's *Taking Shape* is a feast of immanent thinking. It shows that time-worn tools can indeed, when used with patience, sensitivity, rigour, and devotion, yield pleasures rare and contemporary.'

— Mark Truscott, author of *Said Like Reeds or Things*

'Edward Carson's *Taking Shape* is a subtle meditation on love and change, lovers caught up in the changes and rhythms of life on this mortal earth. The elegant couplets repeat phrases, words, and images to hypnotic effect. In a manner reminiscent of E.D. Blodgett's *Apostrophes* — yet entirely its own — *Taking Shape* in its play on repetition and variation traces "the faint/ shape of things taking shape", evoking the weather of love.'

— Hilary Clark, author of *The Dwelling of Weather*

'With evocative imagery and the keen eye of a photographer, Carson gives shape to a language of the heart.'

— Christopher Dewdney, author of *Signal Fires*

'Like ocean tides these words pull and push our logic, hearts and spirit into a communion of evolving spaciousness. *Taking Shape* is powerful and provocative.'

— Lucinda M. Vardey, co-author of *Being Generous* and editor of *God in All Worlds, The Flowering of the Soul*

Taking SHAPE

Edward Carson

The Porcupine's Quill

Library and Archives Canada Cataloguing in Publication

Carson, Edward J., 1948–
Taking shape / by Edward Carson.

ISBN 978-0-88984-305-9 (pbk.)

I. Title.

PS8605.A7776T34 2008 C811'.6 C2008-900347-0

1 2 3 4 • 10 09 08

Cover and interior art: Edward Carson.

Published by The Porcupine's Quill, 68 Main St, Erin, Ontario NOB 1TO. http://www.sentex.net/~pql

Readied for the Press by Wayne Clifford.

Early versions of five of the poems in *Taking Shape* first appeared in the *Danforth Review*.

Represented in Canada by the Literary Press Group. Trade orders are available from University of Toronto Press.

We acknowledge the support of the Ontario Arts Council and the Canada Council for the Arts for our publishing program. The financial support of the Government of Canada through the Book Publishing Industry Development Program is also gratefully acknowledged. Thanks, also, to the Government of Ontario through the Ontario Media Development Corporation's OMDC Book Fund.

ONTARIO ARTS COUNCIL
CONSEIL DES ARTS DE L'ONTARIO

Canada Council for the Arts
Conseil des Arts du Canada

For Joyce

Love is not love which alters when it alteration finds.
—Shakespeare

Love, and do what you will.
— St Augustine

Earth loves the rain; the proud sky loves to give it.
— Marcus Aurelius

The Argument

i

At dawn, the wind we know fans out, full of itself,
taking its shape from all it greets; it calls us outside,

a makeshift voice filtered through our window frame.
Some days, it seeks out the bellies of damp sheets

billowing. Some days, it takes on the white-capping of waves.
Inside, we brace our love against its enticing touch.

We insist on calling our hearts together, and rise into
the day, turning to each other for something to say.

But once outside, we lean cautiously into the wind. The charged
air we breathe breathes into us, prophetic and knowing.

Some days, it seems to be no wind at all — more often, then,
like a swelling of thought. Some days, the wind fans out,

knocking at our door, inviting us into its shape.
Together, we are dimly aware of this inside and out.

Together we are trapped in our own inventions.
What we seem to know best is what we know

to be true, and what we know that is not. There is much
more to learn, and more than we know to leave behind,

but knowing very little, we urge on this new thought
of the gathering wind and the shape of it all around us.

ii

Let loose in the yard, the wind blows like a fearsome sail.
Let loose, it finds a shape like no other. We know

it's a shape with a clear sense of our thinking, a measured
thought, still forming, that takes its place in the world.

Most days, we rise with the wind set free, rise up
and set out, lungs filling with air, in a new direction.

We take comfort in watching the restless waves,
let loose like lies, climb one by one onto the shore.

In the time it takes to rise up, we've uncovered the earth's curve.
The wind is transforming. Our unfinished hearts are shaking.

Most days, the water sprays its light, and the sun hesitates.
The wind says nothing, and nothing moves for fear of moving.

iii

This time around there is no end to history, only the faint
shape of things taking shape, the simple proof of slow

continents reaching out to meet another, touching for the first time.
This time around there is nowhere to go. We ask for nothing

more than the time it takes to take us back in time.
Our history is the only end there is, in itself a wry plot,

an archaeology of love returning and returning to a mortal
shape that betrays its simple elegance and design.

This time around the story will look back on itself. This time
around we will break away from one shape, only to find another.

iv

There is something new to bring home. We know it
to be the liquid white sun rising over our skins.

We wake in the morning with all the gravity of thinking
and doing, with all the love we have to look into.

We imagine ourselves inseparable. We imagine
ourselves held together in a fierce ring of light.

We have each other in mind. We circle the thought
of each other as if it were a place to come home to.

There is no time to think otherwise. There is no time
to remember what shape the earth has become.

You think you are looking out over this world,
but the minute you look — you are not really looking

at the thing you thought that you saw. Now it is every
thing, and nothing more than all you can possibly know.

V

We soon learn to slip free of it. We already
know what begins to take shape is a shifting

of thought. The hard blue bloom of water and sky.
The riot of wind returning — waves leaping up

on a buoy. The angel of white light. And below,
dark merciful fields of mudweed and harbour fish.

Most days the evidence mounts up. The more real
our love seems, the more misleading it must be.

It twists in the wind, this love, finds a path
between the history of our coming and going.

We are here, though not wrapped in each other's arms.
We are here to know what has passed for one thing

and is now another. We inhabit this shape between us,
knowing it has no real name, no sensible place of rest.

The Shape of Things

i

The idle days of autumn close. The planet moves itself
to a place where the thought of everything resides.

This is a place where history lies on its back and dreams.
This is a place where nature has misplaced its urge

to compose itself. The leaves tremble with the shifting earth.
The cooling wind turns itself inside and out.

We lie here beside the open window and wonder what
on earth can keep us from each other. Our sex is a shape

that finds itself taking the shape of the other. In coming
together there is no shape of things to keep in mind,

as if we knew the differences between this way and that.
First comes the hot invention of love, and then the silky stroke

of your bedclothes against me. There is the urgent need to make
sense of our inarticulate breath, our cold sweat, our absent fears.

What takes shape around us is a reflection of words, an island
of knowing one silence, pressed up, hard, against another.

ii

This long night closes. The crimson leaves reach out
to shake themselves free of an incomprehensible darkness.

The shape of things, taking shape, has no final motive.
What we take for one thing can soon fall away

to become another. Understand, then, these knowing
words of ours are one thing now, and another tomorrow.

Minute by minute, the darkest words we can imagine
move silently from one thing to another. We reach

out to each other, only to find no common shape at all.
The argument we are growing has no end in mind,

though even now I dream of our reconciliation,
of running my palm along the sheer nylon heat

of your thigh. A dark space, wholly loving and
surprisingly calm, this darkness we move into.

Not to be denied, this longing, not to be forgotten,
we need to shake this darkness out.

iii

When morning breaks, it does so like a dense tide
moving along a long, flat shore. It does so

with the pace and cadence of a thousand thousand
years of patience and practice, streaming in our window

to find our waking flesh. This might be the glory,
this might be the shape that has no shape at all.

This might be the streaming wind of a wind
that knocks at our door and finds us waiting.

There is everything around us to give us pause.
There is everything around that brings us into

a familiar history of finding this shape of things.
When morning breaks, the dark night surrenders.

The clouds before the sun fill the thoughtful sky,
moving this way, moving that, breathing in, breathing out.

We are careful not to wake everything at once.
We are careful not to find more than one thing at a time.

iv

This water is deep and cold. It needs tasting.
Then, reach out and wrap the water in your arms

and imagine its small pink mouth and tongue
circling your nipple, pulling it in, pulling it out

till you know you just can't take it any more.
This water evades the shape you thought

it might be, fills the suck and glory of your love,
laps in a lick the passion beginning to fill you.

This water fills a dark empty space, admitting its
swelling shape to be whatever you might wish for.

This water has a hold on you that lifts and shakes, brings you
to trembling, soon makes you adore its simple symmetry.

V

The shape of things to come is the very last of things
we think of, the last of a generation of thought

moving between us, inventing the time and place
of our love and memories. Together we will summon

the part of the day, and the part of the night,
the part of the land, and the part of the water

where we have lain so gently in each other's arms,
where we have dreamed so much, and said so little.

There is nothing left on this wide earth to explain.
There is nothing else for us to come home to.

Moving Parts

i

The dark, cold view shows its face on the moon.
We look back at ourselves looking up at the moon.

We look up, and look down, and look right through
to the edge of the earth, to the first snowfall falling.

It's a new shape, this looking back from the moon. It grows
an idea round as the earth, silent and light, and suddenly

we know in our love there is everything to gain, and nothing
to lose. These thoughts are the dark complexities of love,

the miracles of finding space between all and nothing.
In the dark midwinter evening we look south

to catch Venus riding low beneath an even brighter Jupiter.
Their movements are a bold memory of the sky,

a recollection of finding our naked bodies slicing
through the cold white sheets to touch and fondle and lick.

These are the ways of the world, and beyond,
where everything exceeds its reason for being.

ii

This is a time of early snow that finds its deep layers
piled one upon another, laying down the smell of wood

burning to fill the cold penetrating air with sprinkling ashes,
grey and black on the nearby deck and skim of frozen water.

This is a time that drifts in in slow stages, building
on the topsoil thick seams of white awakening, each layer

recalling the shape of a tree, the shape of a rock, finding in each
a measure of memory, a renewal of mortal shape and time.

The unexpected whiteness evades our capture, slips silently by
like a skin shedding its old identity, shaping its new beginning.

iii

The snow-years count up like calculus, a slow, slow glacier
of winters building up and wearing down, moving back

and forth along a curve that shares no common whole.
This is a shape of things that grows beyond the sum

of its parts. This is a geometry of thinking and doing.
My winter comes out of me and brims to the full,

leans over to give you a kiss whole square and deep.
You are full and half by nature, the fragile edge and opposite

of night as is day, black as is white. Our separate passions
number in the thousands, rub the truth out of each other.

I can hold you in my arms, and, at the very first sign
of things to come, make a sign so you will know

how much of a long, long winter this has become,
how wise and dense has gone this velocity of love.

iv

We come to it in steps so small, there is no telling
the centuries it takes for us to find it patiently waiting.

We walk all afternoon to find a simple understanding.
We talk about a quiet calm in which there is no other

thing than the calm itself. There's a moment when,
altogether, the sun and the skim of ice on the lake

are outlines of a shape so perfect that the slow ice
melts. And the speed of that transformation is so

fast, and yet so slow, that the thing that it is
and the thing it becomes, begin and end together.

We come to it in steps so small, walking this way,
slowing our conversation to barely a whisper,

slowing the years that have brought us so far,
slowing the space of one heart beating inside another.

We come to it, barely breathing, slowly … slowly …
The trick is to be so still that no one knows we're moving.

v

Putting things together this way is always something
of a puzzle. The shape of things all seems the same,

so we must find a common name, an element they share.
We stack them shape and colour, beginning with the borders.

We work towards the middle, ignoring the blank
mysterious spaces that seem to have no place at all.

The shape that takes shape begins to look like your mouth,
begins to look like the wisdom of small birds, hesitating

begins to look like something the winter wind said to me,
begins to look like the glory of light returning,

begins to look like a compass of history, the silence of knowing,
begins to look like the shape of things to come.

Memory

i

The earth is gulping down the rain in huge, heavy pools.
Around us, the unpredictable trees catch the clear light

of lightning, a clean iridescent flame, larger than life.
And we, in our love, are lucid as a climate of sleep.

We brood over the tug and pull of our history,
like sleepwalkers, earthbound and walking on air.

Our love is everything it has been, and nothing
more than what it has found to be true.

Our love is the mathematics of dividing this from that,
of finding out there is no other answer possible.

Our love is made to be moved from one place
to another, slow as granite, shapeless as water.

ii

This is either where the wind begins, or, like a memory,
it surrounds the shape of things, thinking it to be so.

We think of a love that becomes the wind, becomes
what you suspect it to be, thinking there is no end

to the way things change, the way one kind of longing
overcomes another, the way believing in you is to be

prepared for seeing in a special way belief, the way
the whole is everywhere that much more than its parts.

We think of a love that becomes the wind.
We think of a longing that thinks no place, no shape

is beyond its reason for being, believes the way
things change is a change in the way of all thought things.

So things are blown together, and apart, piece by piece.
And for us, there is no telling the centuries it will take.

iii

This long, deep love of ours is an impossible thought.
Drifting up like a bubble, shimmering with cause and effect,

it shifts its shape with the energy of oxygen letting loose.
From above, the April moon makes a crescent face.

From below, a dark gravity unties it from our earthly reason.
It floats between us, taking its shape from its freedom.

This wind is an impossible sound that begins, speaking softly.
It speaks no question that is more than we thought, no question

that we can't put together, like parts of a world, like the wave
upon wave of silent continents colliding beneath our feet.

You lean into me with a momentum that will take us
as deep as we can go, farther still than you might imagine.

Our longing is really no place of thought at all. We thought
it was the wind, but it isn't that either. We come away

thinking the thought was one thing, then another. We come
away believing in the shape of something with no shape at all.

iv

We begin with an idea of love that soon becomes something else.
Our words to each other float by like small continents, pulling

away from one clear thought, drifting towards another, caught
in currents so wide and slow we can't resist saying one thing,

and meaning another. We begin with an idea of love that takes
its place in the thought of you. In a perfect world, imagining

you is never enough, remembering in a perfect world there's
more than one way to love each other. Every thought,

in a perfect world, will get us to where we want to be, where
nothing, in a perfect world, is ever so simple as complex.

We can be wise in the ways we think and do, in a perfect world.
I can imagine you more and less than you are, in a perfect world.

So this is our world, more perfect and simple than we might see,
so wisely imagined, made wisely remembered by you and by me.

V

Some things are made to be exactly what they are. Some things
are made more difficult to imagine than the shape of your lips.

Someone will ask, 'What body of thought is made from this hum
of skin?' Some will have answers in mind. Others will not know

what to say, or, in seeing nothing, will say it is what it is. Some
things are made more difficult to see than the open pose you strike,

stretched out upon the bed. Who would have imagined, seeing
you there, what some see before them and others cannot?

Who would have imagined the things that are said, and
those that are not? The whole of this thing might be, then,

a metaphor of love, the thing that is what it is, the thing that now is
exactly what it is that lies between us. Some things are made to be

something opposite and true, made to be one thing after another,
again and again, some love that is now, and some that is not.

Sum of the Parts

i

Turning east and looking into the emptying sky,
did you expect to find something more?

I watch you point into the gathering dark, charting the long
line of clouds stretched thin and flat on the smeared horizon.

You think for a moment there is something more, poised
just beyond your outstretched hand, like a flowing stream

moving freely, a deepening channel of eddies and pools.
You think there is something there to remember, something

only your eyes can see in the expectant stars. From the south,
a plane's white plumes scrawl across the air, draw lines

dividing the setting sun and evening marching on.
All of our instincts, gathering together, want to know

something more than what has brought us here, want
to know where the sun sleeps and full moon spends its days.

ii

Did we look up and see something more? Was it there
long before we arrived, before we'd even thought of it?

You look across to map my gaze, and then turn your back,
knowing my nod is a sign to be ready, a signal to gather

together the shape of our love. From the faraway north
an uncertain breeze curves down, rattling the leaves

in the air, scraping against the tree limbs like dry paper dolls.
In the emptying sky, the starry embrace is streaking towards us.

What remains to be known, in the long night reaching out,
uncertain of its greeting, these visions in the shape of our hearts?

iii

Every thing becomes a version of another. An old song,
crackling, flows out from the radio at dawn, a new map

of voices crooning into the room, a ghosting of airwaves.
It wakes the sleeping birds outside to a soft, naked sound.

Yet, when it comes to our love, we're both in the dark.
We look to appear together, before we have even arrived.

There is no one else we know better, no one we reach for
beyond these four walls who has not looked hard for the other.

Every thing that we think, and all that we say, will intersect,
will join our love's song to above and below, over and under.

And in that clear, clean second, our hands, then and now,
like birds, inside and out, in front of us, touching, this music

filling the air around us, liquid as lightning … Should we
wish for a shape as calm and serene, heard before knowing?

iv

Driving home the thought of our love, the heavy
rain swirls and circles outside in a nervous dance.

At this speed we can escape our shaking hearts,
adding up the long miles, stepping in our uncertain tracks.

Did you ever have the feeling that you wanted to stay?
Did you ever have the feeling that you wanted to go?

What more shall we hope for but this long slow curve
we inhabit, the naked unbroken lines of our lives?

There are more questions following our every turn,
more questions to open and close, press together

until, driving home the thought, we come to a place
so far, so far removed from everything we know.

V

Our love is the one thing it was meant to be, before
our love meant more than what we knew it to be.

Never satisfied, we reach into the heart of the weather, lean
into the darkness around us made as bright as the sun.

The lightning leaves the angry cloud at the same time
it leaves the earth, and we are set free in its furnace.

Both rising and falling, the lightning's voice
is the sound of the void, is a terrible darkness within us

echoing through the starless sky. We soon emerge,
two mirrors of coming and going, neither content

to follow the science of our cause and effect, but frozen,
mesmerized, in the sizzling air and sodden earth.

In a second, our lives become a short history of lightning.
We learn to forget nothing, and let everything go.

We learn to be the sum and minus of this story,
the uncertain edge in the shape of things to come.

Edward Carson is twice winner of the E.J. Pratt Poetry Award in Canada, and is the author of a previously published book of poetry, *Scenes*.

Over the past thirty years he has had a variety of careers involving the word, including co-founder/editor of the literary periodical, *Rune*, and lecturer in English Literature at the University of Toronto. He has served as president of several major book publishing companies, including Penguin Group (Canada), Pearson Technology Group Canada, Distican (Simon and Schuster), HarperCollins Canada, and, while vice president of publishing, founded the successful indigenous publishing list of Random House of Canada.

Throughout his publishing career he taught the business of publishing at Ryerson University, Humber College, and as co-director of the Banff Publishing Workshop. He also has participated on various Boards of Directors, including PEN Canada, BookNet Canada, and is a past president of the Canadian Publishers' Council. At present he is Chief Business Officer and Associate Director, University of Toronto, School of Continuing Studies.

As an editor and publisher, he has worked with an array of accomplished local and international authors, including Carol Shields, Dennis Lee, Marilyn Bowering, John Irving, D.G. Jones, Keith Maillard, Julian Barnes, John Ralston Saul, Barry Lopez, Robert Kroetsch, Eli Mandel and Janice Kulyk Keefer.

Recent showings, and the growing success of his digital photography, have integrated his fascination with the written word and the visual image, expanding the borders and potential for his art (www.photographicart.ca).